Cycling 1

An Anthology of Bicycle Verse

Edited by
Hugh Morrison

Montpelier Publishing
London
2016

ISBN-13: 978-1537373706
ISBN-10: 1537373706
This compilation © 2016 Montpelier Publishing, London.
All rights reserved.

Contents

Up the Hill	Ninon Neckar	1
To My Bicycle	Chris Wheeler	2
Benedicite	S Conant Foster	5
An Ode to Sprinklers	William D Kempton	7
New York Ride	Anon	8
America's Song of the Wheel	Chris Wheeler	9
The Pilgrim	J G Dalton	11
A Morning Ride	Chris Wheeler	12
To my Bicycle	S Conant Foster	13
The Ixion Bicycle Club	Anon	14
A Modern Bicycle	Anon	16
The Cyclometer's Victim	William D Kempton	18
Toasting Song	S Conant Foster	19
The Bicycle Girl	William Hogan	20
Night Lights	Chris Wheeler	21
A Dryland Sailor	Anon	22
A Song of Lancaster Pike	Chris Wheeler	23
An Incident	Anon	24
On the Road	Chris Wheeler	25
Owed to the Bicycle	J G Dalton	26
A Ride at the Close of Winter	Chris Wheeler	27
Unsatisfied	Anon	28
Devon, fair Devon	Chris Wheeler	29
A Midwinter Reverie	S Conant Foster	30
Tightened Spokes	Chris Wheeler	31
Going Downhill on a Bicycle	Henry Charles Beeching	32
The Scorcher	William D Kempton	33
Gearing Down	Anon	34
Bicycle Size	Anon	35
A Would-Be Aeronaut	William D Kempton	36
Rota Felix	J G Dalton	37
In Heaven	William D Kempton	38
To my Bicycle	Anon	39
A Modern Knight	William D Kempton	40
Over the Handles	A S Hibbard	41
The Strike of the Bike	William D Kempton	43
Ting-a-Ling	Anon	44
A Cyclist's Litany	William D Kempton	45

To One of the Bicyclists	Carrie P Richards	46
Out of Wind	William D Kempton	47
The Wheelman	Anon	48
The Reckless Coaster	William D Kempton	49
A Bicycling Idyll	Anon	50
A Spring Poem	William D Kempton	57
On the Road	Ninon Neckar	52
An Epitaph	William D Kempton	53
On Wings of Love	S Conant Foster	54
Rota et Rotula	Abel Elder	56
A Summer's Day	Anon	57
Fair Weather	Anon	58
To My Wheel	Anon	59
The Sociable	George Chinn	60
Bicyclicalisthenics	J G Dalton	62
The Wheel	Anon	63
His First Ride	J G Dalton	64
Punctured	Anon	65
A Centurion	William Carleton	66
On Rainy Days	Anon	67
The Cycle	Anon	68
A-Wheeling	Anon	70
Song of the Cycle	Charles S Crandall	72
The Winter Cyclist	Peter Grant	73
Ho! For the Wheel	Margaret E Sangster	74
Just Mud	Anon	75
The Cyclist's National Anthem	J G Dalton	76

Up the Hill

Up the hill, up the hill —
Surely, though slow;
Work with a ready will;
Steady we go.
We'll rest, lads, we'll rest
When we get to the brow;
There's a time for our work,
And that time, it is now.

Up the hill, up the hill —
Never despair;
The summit is waiting still;
Others are there.
They pedalled, and pedalled
Along, lads, through life;
And now they are watching
Us boys in the strife.

Up the hill, up the hill —
Nearer, more near;
Places are yet to fill
By some now here;
Push on lads, push on —
There are fortunes to choose;
There is plenty to gain,
As there's plenty to lose.

Ninon Neckar

To my Bicycle

My bicycle! My brave old steed!
I would not part with 'thee
Were all the pleasures life could give
Flung in its lap for me;
I would not give the glorious sense
Of joy bound in thy wheel,
For all the vaunted pleasures life
Could, or could not reveal.
For where can I so surely find,
Outside of human kind,
A friend like thee, who never fails
To ease this tired mind?
I only sought in thee for what
My other pastimes yield,
But now, I would not give thee up
For all in pleasure's field.

I love the motion of thy rush,
The cool air coursing free
Away behind, where vanished scenes
Have left their smile with me,
The pulse's throb, the panting breath,
The lazy, lingering stroll,
The leaves of nature's book, which oft
The old dame will unroll;
All speak to me in varied tones,
And tell the same old tale,
They sing the same sweet song that breaks
From wood, and height, and vale —
The same old tale that lives and laughs
Within the streamlet's flow,
The same old song that's softly sung
'Mid trees where breezes blow.

They nourish still my dearest wish,
My wild, untamed desire,
To revel in a life of which
The heart could never tire;

To ramble where, unfettered with
The tramm'ling laws of men,
I find no mark to bid me shun
Rude height or rocky glen.
Yes, thou canst bear me swift to where
In semblance nature still,
Holds sway o'er scenes that once but knew
And owned no other will
Save that, which bade the river run
As it had run before,
Save that which threw no steel track down
Along its level shore.

My brave old 'wheel!' my true old 'wheel!'
Thou'll bear me oft again,
'Mid scenes and sounds that own no rule-
Save that of nature's reign;
The cares that will beset our life,
Born of the strife that brings
To hearts and hands the semblance but
Of fortune's gilded rings,
Are scattered by thy kindly aid,
Are flung where far behind,
They vex no more the heart that yields
Its dearest rights to mind.
The showy tribute wrung from life
By eager, grasping hands,
Is after all but gold foil wrapped
Round griping iron bands;
The shining gleam, the tempting blaze,
Of glory lingering there,
Creeps in at last and crushes out
The life that lives by care.

Then bear me on, my gallant wheel;
No pulse of life may dwell
Within thy limbs of burnished steel,
Which serve thy master well;
But still it seems to me that oft
An answering thrill from thee,

Gives back some free-born fancy, drawn
By nature's touch from me.
Then bear me on, we leave afar
The wheel of human strife
And, listening, hear a voice that whispers,
Cycler, love thy life.

Chris Wheeler

Benedicite

From out the heated city Cyclist takes
His way; an instant pauses at the gates,
An instant listens as the morning wakes
The din of life he leaves behind; then waits
No more, but with a cry of pleasure flees
To where his wheeling song may freely rise
On air more pure; where floats the sweetened breeze
Between the verdant fields and azure skies.

Through woody hollows carpeted with moss.
Up daisy-covered hills, o'er babbling brooks,
Down steep, uncertain paths, with vines across,
In sleep-enticing spots and ivied nooks.
Past cooling caves — from each to each he flies;
Now sinking deep amid some clover bed.
Now drinking crystal dew of summer skies
From out some lily cup above his head.

Upon a cliff, in mute amazement lost,
He stands at last and listens to the roar
And rush of waters, by late tempests tos't,
That crush in anger on a rocky shore.
Below him, up the beach and to the right,
Makes in a cove, one of those sheltered spots
That win a sailor's heart, a cosy bight,
Safe haven for some fifty fishers' cots.

'Tis here, in this secluded fishing town.
Where hollyhocks and china-asters grow
Before the doorways weather-worn and brown.
And o'er the shelly paths their petals strow,
That wandering Cyclist, lulled by moaning sea
And sighing wind, by stormy petrel's scream
And flying mist, reposes 'neath the lea
Of an embedded wreck and dreams his dream.

He sees a narrow street, to him well known,
Where busy men go rapidly along,

With woeful care upon their faces shown;
And lo, he, too, is of the anxious throng
Of hurrying ones; a frown of fretting thought
Sits on his forehead and unrests his eye;
Anon he passes down a sultry court.
Then gains a heated office wearily.

All day without he hears the roar of trade.
Within the hum and noise of labouring clerks;
Below accounts lie waiting to be made;
And though the day is done, yet still he works;
Though temples throb, yet still within this den
He lingers on, companion of dull pain.
Till his hand can guide no more the stubborn pen.
And on his desk he rests a weary brain.

In sleeping Cyclist's breast a sigh now burns;
He wakes; looks long upon the land and sea;
Arises; then to beauteous nature turns
And cries aloud, in joyous ecstasy,
'God bless my wheel! It knows nor care nor strife,
For one day out the ever-coming seven
I run with it far from the hells of life,
To find in nature's handiwork a heaven.'

Now all is silent as the falling dew;
The sun has set; the moon, ascended high.
Doth light the slumbering earth with silvery hue;
A night-hawk gives his solitary cry.
Safe in the confines of the heavenly blue.
Again doth Cyclist leave his day of weal;
And, when the city's gates he passes through,
Once more with joy exclaims, 'God bless my wheel!'

S Conant Foster

An Ode to Ye Ubiquitous Sprinklers

Sprinkle, sprinkle, water-cart,
When I wander where thou art;
If the roads be nice and dry,
Always let the water fly.

When the blazing sun is set.
And the grass with dew is wet,
Then the roads your soul delight,
For they're sloppy all the night.

Then when I am in the dark,
And the mongrels round me bark,
I hardly know which way to go,
On the road you've sprinkled so.

Then, the mud which fills the holes
Through which my spattered cycle rolls,
Makes me hope with all my heart
That from this world you'll soon depart.

William D Kempton

New York Ride

I mount my wheel in the evening gray
For a spin to Harlem, two miles away;
I pass the park with its leafy screen,
That hides the roads we have never seen;
Like at hare and hounds when harking back,
I coast the span of the L road's track,
And over the hollows dipping low
Till I meet the sun in the after-glow.
With a joyous sense I wheel along,
My heart is still singing its sweet, low song;
Harlem is reached, no stop nor stay,
Then she's there at the gate, my winsome May!

Anon

America's Song of the Wheel

Cycling's summons is sounding far
O'er each Commonwealth proud that owns a star,
In the dark blue ground of the banner grand,
That flings its folds o'er our fatherland;
And where'er outflung, unfurled, unrolled,
That summons leaps from each falling fold.

From the hardy land of the wild north breeze,
Where the pine knots blaze and the great lakes freeze,
To the land where cousins in Southern clime
Have strung a new spoke in the wheel of time,
Flies the welcome message which makes us feel,
What a union link is the steed of steel.

And the new spoke fitted in Southern land
Is as firm and true as the New South's hand,
Which has butted that spoke with a Union star,
That was tempered well in the lap of war.
What a mighty bond of peace will steal
O'er the land we love, on the brave old wheel.

From the tide that washes the Empire State,
To the wave that rolls through the Golden Gate,
From Alaska's wilds to the crescent moon,
From the Northland's cape to the South's lagoon,
Flies the wheelman's summons, that near and far,
Makes a union land 'neath a union star.

And that union star o'er the cluster grand,
That in union bound forms the fatherland
Is progress, one hand on the dome above,
The other linked on the earth with love;
Oh! The wheel will link in a long bright chain
The stars which divided might shine in vain.

Let this song be sung to the Northern breeze,
Let its whispers fall among orange trees,
Breathing ever soft o'er the cyclers' way
At the breaking forth or the close of day,
Linking heart to heart, joining hand with hand,
Let the wheel roll on through the fatherland.

Chris Wheeler

The Pilgrim

Give me my bicycle of quiet,
My horse of health to walk upon;
Enough of not pultaceous diet, —
My tin of lubrication;
My hose and breeches (leg's true gauge);
And thus I'll take my pilgrimage.
Then every happy day I beg
More paceful pilgrims I may see.
That have cast off their nags of leg,
And ride a-wheelback, just like me.

J G Dalton

A Morning Ride

Speed thee well, my bicycle, speed thee well, I say,
Swiftly thou shalt bear me o'er the travelled way,
Swiftly by the rambling streams,
Where we watch the yellow gleams
Of the wavelets leaping bright
From dark arches into light,
Seeking, like the ready mind,
In the darkness light to find.

Speed thee well, my bicycle, bear me on, I say,
Let thy wheel revolving chase thought of care away,

Every rustling breeze that blows,
Every breaking beam that glows,
Every form that beauty takes
From Dame Nature when she wakes,
Fairy ferns and forest flowers,
All, my 'wheel,' all — all are ours.

Then away, my bicycle, while I urge thee on,
Thoughts of other days flash by that have long since
gone;
Fondly memory backward trends,
And I see and hear old friends,
See them in the shades that play
Through the leafy curtained way,
Hear them in the breeze that makes
Monotones through bushy brakes.

Chris Wheeler

To My Bicycle

Far swifter than e'er Atalanta flew,
And silent as the working of the mind
Thou glidest, leaving city walls behind
To fly to where — in many a brilliant hue
Beneath the moon's pale light — the sparkling dew
In trembling, scintillating drops is found;
Where odours sweet and fragrant fields abound
And nature breathes to man of life anew.
Amazed, I guide thee, noiseless thing of steel!
Scarce using force to urge thee thro' the night.
Wondering if thou, like me, dost bondage feel,
And find relief in this green-pastured flight;
If thro' thy frame the travelled pleasures reel
Responsive, haply, to mine own delight.

S Conant Foster

The Ixion Bicycle Club

Speed on, with peerless, swift-paced steed,
Show forth your utmost powers of speed
(Why will you wobble)?
Fair damsels note your bird-like flight,
And praise your forms compact and light
(Jerked over the cobble).

E'en fools who scoff the iron horse,
Admire your arrow-darting course
(I fear you'll spill):
Your wheels, like chariot of the sun,
Revolve as driven by Phaeton,
(I'm sure you will).

No eye can trace the speeding spokes,
Responsive to your trained feed's strokes,
('Sprained' they should be).
Like bloodhounds bounding to the fray,
Swift as the eagles for their prey —
(The boys pass ye).

You skim along the wondering earth,
And distance steeds of vulgar birth,
(When they stand still);
You rush through plodding, dusty streets,
The swarming, choking town retreats,
(You've had your fill);

You gain the open, well-kept road,
Dirt rims your wheels, with rubber shod,
(You're soaked in sweat);
You rush the hill and win the crown
Then dash like meteors adown
(Some headers get);

Firm poised; you feel of fear no trace;
The fresh'ning breezes flush your face,
(Your shoes are worn);
Your smallest nerves the motion thrills,
And happiness your bosom fills —
(Your breeches torn).

Past lake, o'er hill, through wood, down vale,
You skim like barks before the gale,
(You're saddle-sore);
Your blood within your veins flows free,
You feel of spirit birth with thee;
(You'll ride no more).

Anon

A Modern Bicycle

(To the tune of Gilbert and Sullivan's 'A Modern Major General')

Now all ye jolly bicyclers that love the steed bicicular
Come lend to me, a moment, your elongated auricular
While I unfold to you some rather queer particulars
About the very model of a modern bicycle.

It was built upon a plan that was really quite stupendous
The skill required in mounting it was utterly tremendous
And should we try to ride it now t'would surely make an
                                                                         end of us
For it was the very model of a modern bicycle.

Its name appears to be so hoary and so mystical
That guesses on this subject are apt to be sophistical
Try British Challenge, Premier, Club, or else, more
                                                   euphonistical
Why call it the very model of a modern bicycle.

It as stated by its owner, with the most extreme audacity,
That it could not be taxed beyond its carrying capacity;
But, in making this remark, he must be lacking in veracity,
Altho' it was the very model of a modern bicycle.

The wheels might be described as being periphrastical,
The saddle mounted on a spring, a little too elastical,
But its owner always spoke of it in terms encomiastical,
As being the very model of a modern bicycle.

Its construction, tho' peculiar, yet admits of great rapidity,
Still, people did not seem to buy it with unusual avidity,
Tho' its rider did describe with remarkable lucidity
This antiquated model of a modern bicycle.

But now as I have about exhausted my vocabulary,
I am forced to put an end to this simple
                                        tintinnabulary,
Or else some irate member of our glorious
                                        constabulary,
Will arrest me and the model of a modern bicycle.

Anon

The Cyclometer's Victim

In a great Western city
Lived a man, tough and gritty,
With a love for cycling intense;
He could climb any grade
That ever was made.
Then boast of feeling immense.

Alas I what a pity
This man, tough and gritty,
At last should be so undone!
A cyclometer prize
Did dazzle his eyes —
He raced like the Dickens and won.

After each long trial
He'd look at the dial.
And say to his friends, 'What fun!'
But still it cried more.
Till he finally swore
He'd start on a century run.

With his cycle beside him
In a heap they did find him,
By the side of the road where he laid;
Then read his cyclometer,
As did the thermometer,
One hundred and one in the shade.

William D Kempton

Toasting Song

Away, dull care, away!
Till night doth bud in day,
Till dawn doth lie
In the eastern sky
With a promise bright and gay;
For Joy is king,
And his subjects sing
To the wheel forever and aye.
Away!

Uncork the wine so red
The grape of France hath bled:
Libations pour
Till our sorrows thaw,
And the ice of life is dead;
Till morning steals
On our glistening wheels,
And the order 'Mount' is said.
Uncork.

Hurrah, my friends, hurrah!
Fast fades the morning star;
The sun doth shine
Like the red, red wine.
And our road runs smooth afar.
Let's fill one up
As a treadle cup —
To ourselves and wheels — ha! ha!
Hurrah!

S Conant Foster

The Bicycle Girl

Of all the girls sweet that I've met on the street,
And thousands of them I have seen,
With beauty so rare and bright golden hair,
The bicycle girl is the queen.
Those dear little creatures with rosy-hued features,
Will set a man's brain in a whirl,
If he stand on the grass and watch them fly past,
That lovely, sweet bicycle girl.

On the boulevard grand, with cycle in hand,
They take a short spin every day,
In couples and groups, wearing gay riding suits,
They pass everything on the way.
There is no use denying the gents are all sighing
For a chance in that gay dizzy whirl,
By the side of her sweet, who rides graceful and neat,
That lovely, sweet bicycle girl.

In the morn, for a lark, thro' meadow and park,
On her nickelplate safety she rides,
Sometimes with a gent, on pleasure she's bent,
As over the highway she glides.
So show me the man throughout the whole land
Who would not enjoy such a whirl,
From start to the finish, with love undiminished,
For the lovely, sweet bicycle girl.

There's a sweet little lass, who rides in our class,
The sweetest dear girl in the land,
And in marriage, you Bee, she has promised to me
Her delicate, lily-white band.
With this beauty of ours, wearing sweetest of flowers,
Off to the church we will whirl;
Down the pathway of life, with her for a wife,
I'll ride with my bicycle girl.

William Hogan

Night Lights

Far on the winding road,
Wavering slow,
What is that flickering,
Fast flitting glow?
Stars softly showing,
Lights shyly glowing.
Through trees where, blowing,
Winds whisper low.

Hark! On the soft breathing,
Half broken breeze,
Tired with blowing through
Leaf-laden trees,
O'er the woods sleeping,
Music comes creeping,
Voices are keeping
Time to the breeze.

Out from the sumac shade
Glide flashing wheels,
Twining through airy spokes
Melody steals;
Cyclers are singing,
Wild notes ringing,
Deep voices flinging up
Music of wheels.

Chris Wheeler

A Dryland Sailor

My cycle-ship's the only ship
That I delight in sailing;
A trim-built clipper for a trip,
Easy to man and to equip,
Nor fears the breezes failing.

I go aloft to steer my craft —
Keep watch as well for breakers.
The mainmast joins the helmsman's haft,
The steering wheel is never aft;
Queer notions of the makers.

I'm skipper and I'm cabin boy,
The first mate and the second;
The hands, 'all told,' that I employ
To navigate my trim-built hoy,
My fins alone are reckoned.

I trim the sails and take the wheel —
My course is seldom wavy;
A frigate of best plated steel,
Ship-shape from figure head to heel,
The gem of the steel navy.

Your cycle-ship now rides the road
Though not at anchor riding;
But scudding on in nautic mode,
Before the wind may 'you be blowed,'
The short leagues gaily gliding.

A brisk and buoyant breeze attend,
When under weigh you find me,
And joyously my cruising end;
My barque to harbour safely send
To the girl I left behind me.

Anon

A Song of Lancaster Pike*

O'er Lancaster's level,
O'er Lancaster's grade,
Uphill and downhill,
By coppice and glade,

By woods whence the light
Of the recreant day,
Long hours ago
Melted slowly away:

Cycle, O cycle!
Come bear me along,
To where in sweet Bryn Mawr
A bird sings a song.

Chris Wheeler

*A road in Delaware, USA

An Incident

A whirl, a rush, the scorcher* flies
Swift past me, as I slowly wheel.
'Come on, I'll do you up,' he cries,
And pangs of envious pain I feel.
For when a man is forty-eight,
And lithe eighteen flings taunt and jeer,
It's hard to be by cruel fate,
And adipose, kept in the rear.

Along about a mile or so,
A glorious coast my spirit cheers,
To think I may so swiftly go,
In spite of heavy weight and years.
And at the bottom of the hill,
I find the scorcher on his head,
He evidently has had a spill—
I'll 'do him up,' in lint, instead!

Anon

* What would nowadays be called a 'lycra lout'.

On the Road

Away we go on our wheels, boys,
As free as the roving breeze,
And over our pathway steals, boys,
The music of wind-swept trees;
And round by the woods and over the hill
Where the ground so gently swells,
From a thousand throats in echoing notes
The songster melody wells.

Along we speed o'er the road, boys —
The road that we love so well;
Those oaks know the whirr of our wheels, boys,
And they welcome the cycler's bell;
And down in the hollow the streamlet flows
In rollicking humour along,
While flinging its wavelets' cadence up
To challenge the cyclers' song.

Above us we feel in the air, boys,
A spirit that's kin with ours —
A spirit that gives to our life, boys,
The brightest of earth's best flowers;
For the health and the strength that are beauty's own,
That are stamped with nature's seal,
Are securely bound and circled round
In the spokes of the flying 'wheel.'

Chris Wheeler

Owed to the Bicycle

It came o'er the sea,
My Cycle to me,
Came thro' sunshine, storm, and snows;
Rubber and steel.
This, the true wheel.
Turns the same where'er it goes.
Tho' fate may frown, so I ride and fall not,
'Tis life on the wing, a life that can pall not.
Thou cam'st o'er the sea,
Bicycle, to me.
Came whence chilly our east wind blows ;
Seas may congeal,
But the true wheel
Turns the same where'er it goes.

Was not the sea
Made to bring thee?
Land for roads and rides alone ?
Once walking slaves,

Cycle us saves, —
Wheel and liberty's all our own.
No fare to pay, no limits to bound us,
The town behind, and the country around us —
Thou cam'st o'er the sea,
Bicycle, to me.
Came thro' sunshine, storm, and snows;
Seas may congeal.
But thy true wheel
Turns the same, where'er it goes!

J G Dalton

A Ride at the Close of Winter

Thus, thus do I leap to the saddle and fly,
While the woods wave their arms where the spring
                                    grasses lie;
E'er enrobing once more in the harmony guise,
In which nature, enveloping, smothers their sighs,
Granting to them instead the soft whispers that fling
Breathings soft as the velvet born leaves of the spring.

Yes! Thus once again will my wheel bear me on,
Each pedal-push bids some dull trouble begone;
Each turn of the wheel to each draw on the bar
Throws a thrill of delight that will leave lying far
In the distance behind, as in life that's gone by,
What remembering we fain would, forgetting, let die.

Chris Wheeler

Unsatisfied

I spin all day from dawn till dark,
Bestriding a phantom pale,
And often I out-rise the lark,
Out-speed the summer gale;
While, whether I halt by a cooling spring,
Or ride with a burning zest,
A face that I know is following,
A voice in my vagrant breast.

She haunts the sunshine and the shade,
The plain, the hill, the stream,
Till I doubt if she be an earthly maid
Or only a young man's dream.
Astray if rapt with the phantoms bright,
My life may be truly blest
When the homing heart of the wheeling knight
Shall possess and be possessed.

Anon

Devon, Fair Devon

Come, cycle! We'll wander together away
As free as the airy pressure
Of the unseen hand that boldly plays
Through the woodland's leafy treasure.
We'll roam where, far in the western sky,
There are signs that the veil of even
Has, creeping far from the city's side,
Dropped down its dark shade o'er Devon.

O Devon! Fair Devon!
Shadows may close over Devon,
But there's light in an eye
That's as deep as the sky —
When it smiles its brightest o'er Devon!

Chris Wheeler

A Midwinter Reverie

Behold the earth enrobed as winter's bride,
Her snowy mantle creaks beneath the heel,
While passing sleighs with merry music hide
The paths whereon we late did ply the wheel.

The frozen brook no longer gurgles by;
No more the fragrant, blooming flower is seen;
The leafless tree stands naked on the sky,
And only treasured memory is green.

No need for Milton's silent hills to speak,
Or written log to happy hours recall;
With kindling eye and pleasure-burning cheek
Full well, full well, we recollect them all.

Those trips a-wheel before the break of day,
The pause to hear the morning songsters sing,
The break of fast on berries by the way,
The thirst assuaged by kneeling to the spring;

The drill, the race, that memorable run,
Quixotic like, in search of conquests fair, —
Each joyed event returns like summer sun,
To warm the chillness of the winter air.

Roll on, ye frosts, and spend your rime and hoar!
O despot winter, sway your substance through!
Full soon the hour when summer reigns once more,
And we enjoy her ecstasies anew.

S Conant Foster

Tightened Spokes

In my wheel there's a spoke that never loosens,
In the handle a bar that never bends,
And so tried and true are these faithful servants
That they hold in my heart the place of friends.

There are spokes in the wheel of time that tighten,
That yield not their hold as the years roll by;
They are mostly thoughts that are linked with the love
Of the friends who now are no longer nigh.

Chris Wheeler

Going Downhill on a Bicycle

With lifted feet, hands still,
I am poised, and down the hill
Dart, with heedful mind;
The air goes by in a wind.

Swifter and yet more swift,
Till the heart with a mighty lift
Makes the lungs laugh, the throat cry —
'O bird, see; see, bird, I fly.

'Is this, is this your joy?
O bird, then I, though a boy
For a golden moment share
Your feathery life in air!'

Say, heart, is there aught like this
In a world that is full of bliss?
'Tis more than skating, bound
Steel-shod to the level ground.

Speed slackens now, I float
Awhile in my airy boat;
Till, when the wheels scarce crawl,
My feet to the treadles fall.

Alas, that the longest hill
Must end in a vale; but still,
Who climbs with toil, wheresoe'er,
Shall find wings waiting there.

Henry Charles Beeching

The Scorcher

Charm'd by the sweet and melodious notes
That pour'd from a score of feather'd throats,
Breathing the hay's delicious scent,
As through the fields my course I bent;
Far down the road I chanced to spy
A man on a wheel which seemed to fly.
As past where I stood, like a rocket he went,

I saw on his face a look so intent;
A look of pain and anxious haste,
That seemed to say, 'No time must I waste,'
For blind and deaf to nature's display,
With downcast eyes he sped on his way.
'It must be a case of life and death,'
I said to myself with bated breath;
'At the door of death some dear one is laid,
And he doth haste for medical aid.
Oh fly, thou wheel, with the wings of the wind.
That he that aid may speedily find,
And again to health that lov'd one restore.
Hasten, I pray thee, beg, and implore.'

Alas, my friends, it was all a mistake,
He was only trying a record to break.
He rode like a fool, and never once stopp'd
Till, his heart giving out, from his wheel he dropp'd
And gave up the ghost on the ground where he lay.
But he beat the record three seconds, they say.

William D Kempton

Gearing Down

All, for comfort who incline
And for easy riding pine
List to him who pens this line —
'Gear them down.'

Then as thro' the countryside
Effortless almost, you glide
In the cool of even tide
'Well geared down.'

Bless the day when first you heeded
This the counsel surely needed
By the riders of the 'speeded' —
'Gear them down.'

Anon

Bicycle Size

If for safety you aspire
And your muscles would not tire
Ride well within your reach
Is the motto I would teach.

If you ride the largest size
You can reach by stretch of thighs,
Your calves you'll surely strain,
And repent when on the train.

If headers you would get,
Heed not my counsel yet;
But when out upon your wheel,
Down with toe and up with heel.

If your pedal you like to slip,
And to earth would touch thy lip,
Ride the very biggest wheel
That a pointed toe can feel.

Anon

A Would-Be Aeronaut

Said a lad who aspired to be a high flyer,
As he saw a wheel with a pneumatic tire,
High o'er the heads of the crowd I could pass,
If the tires were but filled with hydrogen gas.

Straight to the store of the dealer he hies.
And picks out a tire of generous size,
And to further assure the success of his plan,
He adds a monster electrical fan.

When the tires were inflated with hydrogen gas.
The curious public assembled en masse
To see him start on his trip to the skies
And he strained every nerve to make the thing rise-
But it wouldn't.

William D Kempton

Rota Felix

Come, Wheel, and with thy fleet reprieving.
Rock me in delight awhile;
Let some pleasing roads beguile
My reflections, so from thence
They may take an influence
All my sours of care relieving.
Though but a skeleton a-gliding,
Life it brings for man or boy!
Walkers suffer long annoy,
Ill content with any thought
In their laggard fancy wrought:
Be mine the joys that come of riding!

J G Dalton

In Heaven

'What kind of streets does heaven have?'
Said Johnny to his mother;
'Say, are they hilly, rough, or smooth,
And one just like another?'

'They're paved with purest gold, my son.
And level as a table;
They're smooth as polished glass, you'll find,
If you'll but read the Bible.'

'Then if I'm good as I can be,
And die and go to heaven,
Say, can I ride a golden wheel
Upon those streets so even?'

'Oh, no, my son, the people there
Will spend their time in singing.
And forevermore that blest abode
With anthems will be ringing.'

'Well, if I go there when I die,
And riding is forbidden,
I'll ask the man who keeps the gate
To let me out of heaven.'

William D Kempton

To My Bicycle

O gleaming mesh of steel, to me
Thou art indeed a mystery.
Thy lofty perch I stride, content,
While people gaze in wonderment,
And poets chant in roundelays
Thine airy form and bird-like ways.

How fleetly dost thou bowl along —
All quiet save the merry gong —
Past field and wood and lake and brook,
Through shady dell, by cosy nook.

The bee drones in the waving grass,
Nor stops his humming as we pass;
The daisy nods in modest glee,
The bird sings gaily in the tree,—
All nature smiles in gladness bright,
While on we wing in rapid flight.

Wherever fancy turns we glide, —
Through dusty town, by ocean's side;
With light and joyous feelings rife,
Thou seem'st a very thing of life.

Thy potent charm around me cast
Binds me to thine allurements fast.
Ah, wheel! Such is thy magic spell,
Resistance is impossible.

Anon

A Modern Knight

In books which are yellow and musty with age,
We read of knights who were fearless and brave;
Who wore iron clothes and rode fiery steeds,
And cut short the life of many a knave.

This knight of ours was not one of those.
His steed had four legs, yet 'twas fashioned from wood.
He bestrode it at morn, dismounted at eve.
Yet it never once stirr'd from the spot where it stood.

His lance was a pen well poisoned with ink,
Which he skilfully used with such fatal effect
That his fame spread abroad, and wherever he went
He was sure to be met with the greatest respect.

Alas, for our knight! His triumph was brief.
For a legion of imps his weapon defied.
Though he fought them with powders and queer little
                                                               pills
And every concoction he heard of was tried.

He fought them in vain and began to despair.
When someone suggested he try a new steed.
He took the advice and purchased a wheel.
And no longer's a prey to the pharmacist's greed.

William D Kempton

Over the Handles

One day I was riding my wheel so free,
Toward the garden wall;
A charmer was standing and looking at me,
From over the garden wall.
Her face was fair
So saucy her air,
I was rattled completely
And right then and there
I took a bad header
And flew through the air
Over the garden wall.

Chorus:
Over the garden wall,
A terrible, terrible fall;
I never did yet
A header get
That filled my soul
With such regret,
As the time I struck
Head-first in the wet
Over the garden wall.

I picked myself up and said 'How do you do?'
Over the garden wall.
She said 'I'm certainly better than you.'
Over the garden wall;
'But much I should like,
To know why you strike,
And get so hot, and muddy, and dusty like,
And take such a header from off your bike,'
Over the garden wall.

Chorus: Over the garden wall, etc.

'My dear,' said I, 'I can surely explain,'
Over the garden wall;
'The case in a moment, if I may remain,'
Over the garden wall;
'Your glance was so shy,
I wished to be nigh,
So over the handles I went with a fly!
But now I beware of a saucy black eye,'
Over the garden wall.

A S Hibbard

The Strike of the Bike

Though science may teach, and experiment prove
That pain is unknown to iron and steel,
Yet a tale which I heard and will shortly relate
Constrains me to think that at least they can feel.

It concerns the fate of a weak-minded lad,
Whose consuming desire was a record 'to beat,'
Who liv'd on his wheel, and though urged by his friends
'Twas seldom he'd leave it to sleep or to eat.

He rode till even the wheels were tir'd,
The down-trodden pedals complain'd of their lot,
The many-link'd chain rebell'd at the strain
And the bearings had grown exceedingly hot.

When forbearance and patience had come to an end,
They sought out some means to vent their dislike,
And after discussing this plan and that
They firmly resolved to go on a strike.

He kept on his way and was nearing the goal.
He flew like the wind and was bent o'er his work,
For he had but a very few seconds to spare.
When lo! His wheel was stopped with a jerk.

He slid o'er the handles and lit on his head,
His friends gather'd round to look at the wreck.
The wrongs of the 'bike' at last were avenged,
For instead of the record he'd broken his neck.

William D Kempton

Ting-a-Ling

Oh listen to the music of the bells, cycle bells.
What a tale of happiness their harmony foretells;
How they tinkle, tinkle, tinkle, in the frosty air of night,
While the glistening pedals twinkle in the silvery
                                  moonbeams light,
Keeping time, time, time, in a bicycular rhyme,
To the tintinabulations of the bells.

Anon

A Cyclist's Litany

From those who carry no oil for their wheels,
Yet always bother us
And drain our cans of the very last drop —
'Good Lord, deliver us!'

From those who ask to try our wheels,
And then will anger us
By riding full tilt over ruts and stones —
'Good Lord, deliver us!'

From those who ride the 'only' wheel,
And are wont to pester us
By singing its praises for hours and hours —
'Good Lord, deliver us!'

From the potmetal* wheel, though warranted steel,
Is sure to break under us
Just when we are miles and miles from home —
'Good Lord, deliver us!'

From these and a thousand kindred ills
Which still hang over us
And threaten to make us crabbed and cross —
'Good Lord, deliver us!'

William D Kempton

To One of the Bicyclists

Come forth on your bicycle, Charlie,
And ride, while I gaze and admire;
But if you won't think it presuming,
I wish you would change your attire.

Your legs are a trifle too thin, dear,
To be so exposed to the light,
So won't you just pull down your trousers,
And keep them wrapped up out of sight?

Your face is so noble and manly,
Your shoulders are well set, and square,
And with such a splendid beginning,
Those spindles but poorly compare.

You just make me think of a story
(You see I must tell you the worst),
About the old man in the Bible,-
Whose last end was worse than the first.

So take my advice now, dear Charlie,
And keep those legs nicely concealed,
And people won't dream they're so scraggy,
In judging by what is revealed.

But come on your bicycle, Charlie, —
Your riding I really admire,
And when you have wrapped up those pipe-stems,
You're all that my heart could desire.

Carrie P Richards

Out of Wind

When I learn'd to ride a wheel
I often was chagrin'd
To find, before I'd ridden far,
That I was out of wind.

I therefore bought a brand new wheel,
With tires that you inflate.
And hoped this trouble to avoid —
But such was not my fate.

A piece of wire ran in that tire
On which my faith I'd pinn'd,
And again I found I could not ride
Because I was out of wind.

William D Kempton

The Wheelman

The coach and car I like nor loathe,
Extremes are suited not for all;
On steely bike, unlike them both,
I surest sit and fear no fall.
This is my choice; for me I feel
No ride is like the quiet wheel.

I grind no scissors, turn no mill,
I bear no goods of any trade;
I skim the plain, I climb the hill,
But greatest cities I evade,
And laugh at them in care and pain
Who barter health for golden gain.

Come up betimes, thou heavy wight,
That keep'st the lower ways of brick!
Rise now and walk the wires light,
While not too old to travel quick.
Take to the saddle ere too late, —
True life goes with the rapid gait.

Anon

The Reckless Coaster

With faith in his luck, without bound,
No coast too steep could be found;
But he struck a cart end
As he swept 'round a bend,
And his spirit leap'd out through the wound.

At 'head work' he was quite an adept;
He knew all the tricks of the track,
From ankle motion to final spurt,
Did this wonderful racing crack.

They could not pocket him, he said.
For he always rode very wide;
But the man who won, like the Levite of old.
Passed by on the other side.

William D Kempton

A Bicycling Idyll

A little girl, with eyes of blue;
A little dog of snowy hue;
A little wheel, with rider rash;
A bark, a rush, an awful crash!

A little scream; a little swear;
A pretty sympathetic air;
A little conservation, leading
To blushes, smiles, successful pleading.

A little church; a little bride;
A gallant wheelman by her side;
A little kiss, their vows to seal;
A little rival for the wheel.

Anon

A Spring Poem

Spring, spring, of well temper'd steel.
Absorbing the jolts that we'd painfully feel,
Of chanting thy praises we never shall tire,
Thou gentle hand-maid of the pneumatic tire.

A source of pleasure for age and for youth,
A boon for man and woman, forsooth.
Our mem'ry shall cling as long as we live
To the freedom from jar that thy advent didst give.

William D Kempton

On the Road

Away we go on our wheels, boys,
As free as the roving breeze,
And over our pathway steals, boys,
The music of wind-swept trees;
And round by the woods and over the hill
Where the ground so gently swells,
From a thousand throats in echoing notes
The songster melody wells.

Along we speed o'er the road, boys, —
The road that we know so well;
Those oaks know the whir of our wheels, boys,
And they welcome the cycle's bell;
And down in the hollow the streamlet flows
In rollicking humor along;
While flinging its wavelets' cadence up
To challenge the cycler's song.

Above us we feel in the air, boys,
A spirit that's kin with ours,
A spirit that gives to our life, boys,
The brightest of earth's best flowers;
For the health and strength that are beauty's own,
That are stamped with nature's seal,
Are securely bound and circled round
In the spokes of the flying wheel.

Ninon Neckar

An Epitaph

When Death puts forth his clammy hand
And claims me for his own,
Pray dig my grave in a quiet spot
And o'er it place a stone.

Engrave thereon a winged wheel,
And then, beneath, inscribe:
'He loved the wheel, and never tir'd
It's pleasures to describe.'

William D Kempton

On Wings of Love

Freshets rushing,
Bridges crushing,
Stay the way of
Train and team —
What bold stranger
Braves the danger?
Who doth cross yon
Angry stream?

Strongly, swiftly,
Deeply, deftly.
Dip his paddles
In the tide;
Bravely done, sir!
Nobly won, sir!
See! He gains the
Other side.

Wheel he carries,
Waits nor tarries,
Mounts, and quickly
Rolls away;
While in wheeling.
Joyous feeling
Vents in happy
Roundelay.

"Cycle, 'cycle.
Whirling 'cycle,
Tell thy rider,
An' thou please.
What sweet saying
Love betraying,
Thou dost whisper
To the breeze.

'Nay, my beauty,
'Tis thy duty
To unfold thy
Wisdom. Come!
Voice thy learning
To thy turning;
What! In whisper
Still art dumb?

'Rogue of metal!
Leaf and petal.
Twig and shrub on
Either side;
Wondering prattle,
As we rattle;
Tell them why we
Swiftly ride.

'On! O 'cycle!
Knavish 'cycle
Churl to make thy
Master speak;
On to meet her!
On to greet her!
On! till journals
Smoke and creak.

Mark! O 'cycle!
From St. Michael
Tolls th' appointed
Hour of four:
Hurry! Speed ye!
Fly! For heed ye,
She doth signal
From the door.'

S Conant Foster

Rota et Rotula

When life is lazy in my veins
And joy is gone away,—
Although my legs' November lacks
The spring'ness of their May,
I climb and scamper off on that
Will warm my heart to move;
'Tis greater wheel and lesser wheel,
On the pleasant seat above.

The guiding wand of silver hue,
The spinal hollow bright,
With shapely shanks that play or rest
Like creatures of delight;
Oh, these combine a stir and shine
To warm old hearts to move
By greater wheel and lesser wheel,
On the russet seat above.

The great white wheel, I tread it as
Switzer his mount of snow,
And much the good me there befell
That many more can know;
For a quiet sort of kindling stuff
To warm your heart to move,
Take greater wheel and lesser wheel,
On the pleasant seat above.

Abel Elder

A Summer's Day

A summer's day,
With flowers richly blooming;
The hours drone away
In soft, enchanting dreams.
Sweet grasses and blossomed trees
The heavy air perfuming;
While a southern gentle breeze
Ripples the idle streams.

And then refreshing eventide,
That choicest cycling hour,
When silently I glide
Through cooling wooded glades;
The vista of western clouds,
Which stately elms embower,
With richest golden light enshrouds
The sun which sinks and fades.

A sense of rest the earth o'erspreads,
And fills the world with blest content;
While in the sky a soft light sheds
From stars that one by one outsteal.
There cannot be too high a praise
Of such a time so happily spent;
Life centres in those halycon days,
Those happy days a-wheel.

Anon

Fair Weather

A bicycler fair, a bicycler brave,
Slowly riding together;
But though he an answer seems to crave,
He's not discussing some subject grave,
But talking about — the weather.

'Cloudless above us spread the skies,
Foretelling glorious weather;
Cloudless, too, are your sweet eyes:
In their depths my future lies,
As we ride together.

'In your eyes, unclouded blue,
Ah! I wonder whether
I might find an omen, too,
I might gain assurance true
Of my life's fair weather?'

Ended now his murmur low,
Still they ride together;
As the shadows longer grow,
On her face a rosy glow
Promises fair weather.

Anon

To My Wheel

No ode I sing to balmy spring,
Though joyful at its coming
As any bird that it will bring
To make the woods and meadows ring
With melody or drumming!

But of my wheel, my bonnie wheel,
I cannot keep from singing,
For it hath made me know and feel
The joy that health and strength reveal,
And pleasure in their bringing.

Thou'rt staunch and true, O wheel of mine
What hours we've known together!
When roads were fair and days were fine?
Aye! When the sun refused to shine,
And stormy was the weather!

When lightning lit the glist'ning way —
The darkness quick succeeding,—
A lurid, tremulous, blinding day, —
Then deepest night— about us lay,
As onward we went speeding.

Companions, daily, to and fro,
Toward rest or labor faring,
As through the busy streets we go,
Other will thou canst not know
Than his whom thou art bearing.

From head-nut unto back wheel cone,
Thy smooth and burnished steel
Fault or blemish ne'er hast shown!
Steed of my choice art thou alone,
My swift, my beautiful wheel!

Anon

The Sociable*

Through the by-way bowling
Silvery night in June;
Wheels so airy rolling
Out a merry tune.

On the cushions resting,
Not the least afraid,
By an interesting
Youth reclines a maid.

Gentle, shy and winning,
Form of willowy grace,
And the night is spinning
Over her fair face

Gauzy web of shadows,
Shot by moonbeams bright,
'Tis to this the lad owes
Half his bliss tonight.

In her ear he whispers
Gaily loves's sweet tale;
Naught she checks the lisper's
Words, as through the dale

Wing they on so fleetly —
Now adown the glade,
Brake he presses fleetly,
And the lithesome maid.

Joys more indolently
With the pedals light;
See them, consequently,
Much retard their flight.

Past the sparkling river,
Green boughs overhung —
Where the rushes quiver,
Breezes soft among.

While from the garden closes,
Incense - breathing rare
Steals the scent of roses
On the evening air.

Happy are the lovers,
As they onward go;
Cupid, near them hovers —
Evening of woe.

Ah, light hearted riders,
Ever may you roll
Through life's vale as gliders
Round a smoothened goal.

George Chinn

*a type of bicycle where the riders sit side by side.

Bicyclicalisthenics

O graceful one that fleetest on, thy pace
Is an aerial promenade, and thy form
Goes poised as if it floated on the air,
With the soft ambulating gait of one
Who timeth all his motions to a measure!
And has Prometheus, say, has he again
Been stealing fire from Helios' chariot-wheels
To light bicycles with, and make them spin?
Who thinks of bicycling hath already taken
One step upon the way to eminence:
Such altitudes delight me — I will launch
On the sustaining wire, nor fear to fall
Like Icarus, nor serve myself like him
Who drove awry Hyperion's fiery steeds.

O fortunate, O happy day,
When a new cycle bears its load
Among the myriad wheels of earth;
Like a young moon just spun to birth.
It rolls on its harmonious way
Into the boundless realms of road.

J G Dalton

The Wheel

'Whither, on whirling wheel?
Whither, with so much haste.
As if a thief thou wert?'

'I have the Wheel of life;
Soiled with my city's dust.
From the struggle and the strife
Of the narrow street I fly
To the Road's felicity,
To clear from me the frown
Of the moody toil of town.'

Anon

His First Ride

Earth with its slow and tiresome ills
Recedes some feet away;
Lift up your heads, ye neighbouring hills,
I'm coming out your way!

My soul is full of pilfered song,
Highwayman's is my right;
Bicycles that I feared too long,
Are things of life — and light.

My pulses fast and fearless beat.
My limbs seek wider bounds,
I feel grow firm beneath my feet
The rubber pedal rounds.

This is the safe and narrow way —
The wires sing in the wind —
To men on horse of flesh I say,
I've no such carnal mind.

In palace-cars I would not be,
Where rides the railroad king;
O steam, where is thy victory?
O bird, where is thy wing?

J G Dalton

Punctured

The preacher spoke of little things.
Their influence and power.
And how the little pitted speck
Made all the apple sour.

He told how great big sturdy oaks
From little acorns grew.
And how the tiny little stone
The burly giant slew.

But the cyclist sat there unimpressed
By all the speaker's fire.
Until he went outside and found
A pin had pierced his tire.

Anon

A Centurion

He tumbled from his weary wheel,
And set it by the door;
Then stood as though he joyed to feel
His feet in earth once more;
And as he mopped his rumpled head
His face was wreathed in smiles;
'A very pretty run,' he said,
'I did a hundred miles!'

A hundred miles!' I cried. 'Ah think!
What beauties you have seen!
The reedy streams where cattle drink.
The meadows rich and green.
'Where did you wend your rapid way —
Through lofty woodland aisles?'
He shook his head. 'I cannot say —
I did a hundred miles!'

'What hamlets saw your swift tires spin?
Ah, how I envy you!
To lose the city's dust and din
Beneath the heaven's blue;
To get a breath of country air.
To lean o'er rustic stiles!'
He only said: 'The roads were fair —
I did a hundred miles!'

William Carleton

On Rainy Days

What though the rain weeps down the pane,
And all the streets are muddy gray.
And cycling hopes are worse than vain
This wet, unhallowed, dismal day —
Still shall my soul know joy and peace.
And sweet delight shall thrill my heart.
As, armed with rags and wrench and grease,
I take by bicycle apart.

One half the pleasure, I opine,
Which focuses upon a wheel
Is that ecstatic and divine
Enjoyment I am wont to feel
When I remove the nuts, or screw
The saddle off, or loose the chain,
Or pull the inner tube to view.
And try to put it back again.

I love to tinker with the forks —
To readjust the mud-guard strips —
To cut deft patches out of corks,
Wherewith to mend the handle-grips;
I take the bearings out, and clean
Them with a piece of an old sack,
And I am happy and serene
Until I seek to put them back.

Oh, rainy days do fill my heart
With rapture which I deem sublime,
For then I take my bike apart,
Just as I did the other time;
I file and rub and twist and chop,
And wrench and pull and paint and scrape.
And next day take it to the shop,
And have it put back into shape.

Anon

The Cycle

I fly from the heat of the noisy street
To the shade of the country lane;
I bear the clerk from his office dark
To the sunny fields again.
On me bestrid, the town-bred kid
May hear the brooklet sing.
And chase the wopse through the leafy copse
Till he finds that the wopse can sting.

I silently glide to mark the tide
Come in on Sandymount strand.
And linger near to the Merrion Pier
If there happens to be a band.
In holiday time more frequently I'm
En route for a longer run;
Up slick and away for Killiney or Bray,
And home with the setting sun.

My frame they rack on the racing track,
And bend each slender spoke;
But little they care how cycles fare
If the record is only broke.
Then, with tightened chain, I am at it again
Till my rider has got too stale.
Or I chance to collide, or I run too wide,
And smash myself up on a rail.

I bring good health, and if not wealth.
Still a saving in cab or car.
And tram and train are ne'er needed again
When you grasp my handlebar.
On a drop of oil I merrily toil,
And need no ostler's care,
Though, of course, when I'm wrecked, you may always
                                                        expect
A pretty long bill for repair.

Of my advent I tell with the clanging bell—
I startle the slumbrous swine;
The ducks stand aghast, and the hen flees past
From those glittering wheels of mine,
Like lightning I dart by the polo cart
Which follows me with a will,
But it's left far behind, except when I find
That the road is all uphill.

You can ride, you're aware, on my tires of air
With never a jolt nor jar;
You can get up the steam and coast like a gleam
Of light from a falling star.
From the town, with its grime, I fly to a clime
Where the beauties of nature are rife;
I'm all you desire and all you require
To make you contented with life.

Anon

A-Wheeling

Have you never felt the fever of the twirling, whirling wheel.
Of the guiding and resisting of the shining cranks of steel;
Never felt your senses reel
In the glamour and the gladness of the misty morning sky,
As the white road rushes toward you, as the dew-bathed
                                              banks slip by.
And the larks are soaring high?

Never known the boundless buoyance of the billowy,
                                               breezy hills,
Of the pine scents all around you, and the running,
                                               rippling rills
Chasing memory of life's ills;
Dashing, flashing through the sunshine, by the windy
                                               wold and plain.
The distant blue heights luring, onward, upward, to the
                                                 strain
Of the whirling wheels' refrain?

Fled from prison, like a prisoner, sped the turning,
                                             spuming wheel.
Changed the city's stir and struggling, jar and vexing,
                                             none can heal.
For the peace the fields reveal.
And with spirit separate, straining above the town's
                                             low reach.
Found a tender satisfaction, which the steadfast summits
                                               teach?
In their silence— fullest speech.

Never known the wistful, wand'ring back, in pleasurable
                                               pain?
Met the kine from milking sauntering to pastures sweet
                                             again.
Straggling up the wide-marged lane?
You have never felt the gladness, nor the glory of the
                                             dream

That exalts, as tired eyes linger still on sunset, mead and stream?
Haste, then! Taste that bliss supreme.

Anon

Song of the Cycle

This is the toy, beyond Aladdin's dreaming.
The magic wheel upon whose hub is wound
All roads, although they reach the world around,
O'er western plains or orient deserts gleaming.

This is the skein from which each day unravels
Such new delights, such witching flights, such joys
Of bounding blood, of glad escape from noise.
Such ventures beggaring old Crusoe's travels.

It is as if some mighty necromancer,
At king's command, to please his lady's whim.
Instilled such virtue in a rubber rim
And brought it forth as his triumphant answer,

For wheresoe'er its shining spokes are fleeting
Fair benefits spring upward from its tread.
And eyes grow bright and cheeks all rosy red.
Responsive to the heart's ecstatic beating.

Thus youth and age, alike in healthful feeling.
And man and maid who find their paths are one
Crown this rare product of our century's run
And sing the health, the joy, the grace of wheeling.

Charles S Crandall

The Winter Cyclist

A wintry chill is in the atmosphere,
As from the heaving lake the storm wind blows;
And weak-kneed brethren of the cycle fear
That brings the riding season to a close.

Jack Frost assails us with his wicked thrusts;
Our polka-dotted mufflers are on guard;
And many a good wheel in the basement rusts
Which should be speeding down the boulevard.

And shall we Join the patient, suffering throng,
Which crowds the rumbling street cars to the door?
Which kicks against the service loud and long,
But keeps on riding as it did before?

Nay! Perish such a thought. On every street
The hardy wheelman has the right of way;
No ancient female comes to claims his seat;
No cable breaks, no lumbering teams delay.

Our hearts beat high, our life-blood dancing flows.
Though ice-flakes sparkle in the biting air;
While street-car heaters, every patron knows,
Are but a vain delusion and a snare.

The steed that bore us through the woods aglow
With sunshine, where the morning glories creep.
Will bear us safely through the mud-streaked snow
Until it lies at least five inches deep.

Peter Grant

Ho! For the Wheel

It's ho! for a ride in the open,
With the cool winds blowing free.
And nothing but joy on dale and hill
For my trusty wheel and me.
It's ho! for the dew of the morning
That sparkles on leaf and spray,
And ho! for the charm of the sunset light
When the glad day fades away.

With muscles that answer quickly
To call of the resolute will,
With cheeks that glow and eyes that shine
And pulses that bound and thrill,
I fly through the beautiful kingdom
That beckons my wheel and me.
Queen of the world of girlhood,
And sovereign of all I see.

Margaret E Sangster

Just Mud

Mud, mud, mud,
As far as the eye can see.
And I'm glad that my tongue can't utter
The thoughts that arise in me.

O well for the city chap
As he rides on the level street.
And well for the country lad
That he's bom with large web-feet.

And the half-filled carts go on,
With a little jag of a load,
But O just to feel the joy of a wheel
And a nice, hard, level road.

Mud, mud, mud.
As far as the eye can see,
But the joy I miss on a road like this
Can never come back to me.

Anon

The Cyclist's National Anthem

(To the tune of God Save the Queen/
My Country 'tis of Thee)

Bicycle, 't is of thee,
Fleet car of levity.
Of thee I sing:
Wheel I and brothers ride.
And on the still rim's pride.
Up every high hill-side
Drive the great ring.

Two-wheeler — or if three.
Car of hilarity,
The same I love;
I hate the rocky ills
That give me ugly spills,
Yet my heart rather thrills —
See as above.

Our bicycle, to thee,
Angel of wheelery,
To thee we sing:
Long make our band be bright
With wheeldom's rolly light ;
Propel us by thy might,
Great pedal king.

J G Dalton

Also available from Montpelier Publishing

The Slow Bicycle Companion
Inspirational quotes from cycling's golden age

Compiled by Hugh Morrison

This book celebrates the golden age of cycling, before the noisy arrival of the motor car and the heavy goods vehicle, when lycra, hi-viz and plastic hats were unknown, bicycles had no brakes let alone gears, and tweed-clad riders puffed on cigars as they pedalled along peaceful country lanes.

If you are a fan of the Slow Bicycle Movement and wish to return to a less hurried, more civilised, and perspiration-free style of cycling, this book of quotations will inspire and amuse in equal measure.

ISBN-10: 1505819474 ISBN-13: 978-1505819472
Available from Amazon in ebook and paperback

Printed in Great Britain
by Amazon